AN EASY-READ COMMUNITY BOOK

WHAT IS A COMMUNITY?

BY CAROLINE ARNOLD

PHOTOGRAPHS BY CAROLE BERTOL

Franklin Watts
New York/London/Toronto/Sydney
1982

Special thanks are due the following individuals and organizations whose cooperation made the photographs possible:

Louise Ferrara and family; Alice McVicker; Jerry Popplewell; Saint Joseph City Council.

R.L. 1.9 Spache Revised Formula

Library of Congress Cataloging in Publication Data

Arnold, Caroline.
What is a community?

(A Easy-read community book)
Includes index.
Summary: Surveys the various elements, character-
istics, and needs of communities which are composed of
families living in neighborhoods.
1. Community—Juvenile literature. [1. Community
life] I. Bertol, Carole, ill. II. Title. III. Series.
HM131.A74 1982   307   82-8602
ISBN 0-531-04444-0   AACR2

CONTENTS

Your Community

Communities are people who live together.

Many people may live in a community. Or just a few.

Your community is the place where you live. Your community is part of your city or town, your state, and your country.

Many people live together in families.

Families share the same living place. They eat together. And they have fun together.

There are many kinds of families.

A mother and father may have one child. Or they may have many children.

A family may have only one parent.

Grandparents, aunts, and uncles may also be part of the family.

What kind of family do you have?

Your family lives in a neighborhood.

Your neighbors are the people who live near you. They may live next door. Or they may live down the road.

In country neighborhoods people live far apart. They must go to a nearby town for many of the things they need.

In city neighborhoods people live close together. Most of the things they need are nearby.

Some people live in suburbs.
Suburbs are at the edge of big cities.
People who live in suburbs may work in
the city.

Each Community Is Different

A city or town has many neighborhoods. Each neighborhood is different.

Each city and town is different, too. Some are big. Some are small. Some are old and some are new.

Communities have different kinds of buildings, weather, and landscape.

What kind of people live in your community?

People have different colors of hair, eyes, and skin. They may be short or tall. They may be fat or thin. They may be young or old.

Some people in your community may speak a different language. They may do things in different ways.

People live in many kinds of houses, wear many kinds of clothes, and like different things.

What kind of weather do you have in your community? Does it rain? Does it snow? Some communities have lots of fog. Some have lots of sun.

Each community has its own kind of weather.

What does your community look like?

Is it flat or hilly? Is it near a lake, a river, or the sea? Is it near forests or on a plain?

Each community has a different landscape.

Communities Change

What was your community like 10 years ago? What was it like 100 years ago?

Look at the buildings in your community. Are they old or are they new?

When buildings get old they wear out. They may be torn down. But sometimes old buildings are saved. The worn out parts are fixed. Old buildings can help us remember our past.

New buildings look toward the future. People try to make new buildings better than old ones.

People in communities change, too.

People get older. Children grow up. New children are born.

People move from one community to another.

Have you ever moved?

Sometimes people move from one part of a city to another.

Sometimes people move to a new town or city or to the country.

Sometimes people come here from other countries. They bring some of their customs with them. Those customs become part of the community.

Doing Things Together

People in communities do things together.

People in communities go to school. Small children, big children, and adults all go to school.

Do other children in your community go to your school? Or do they go to a different one? Many communities have more than one school.

People in communities work and play together.

There are many kinds of jobs in each community. Each job provides something that people need.

What kind of job does your mother or father do?

Do you know what kind of work you want to do when you grow up?

People in communities shop together.

Everybody needs food and clothing. People need to buy other things, too.

Sometimes you can shop in your own neighborhood. Sometimes you may go to a shopping center or a supermarket.

Where do you usually go to shop?

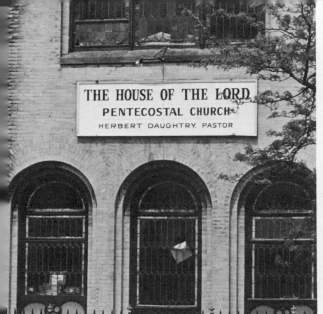

People in communities worship together.

In our country people may worship in their own ways. Some worship in churches. Some worship in synagogues. Some worship in other ways.

People in Communities Need Things

People in communities need water and energy.

We all need water to drink, to cook, and to wash. Farmers need water for their plants and animals.

In most towns and cities water goes through pipes to where people live. In some places people must dig wells to find water.

We all need to have clean water, clean air, and clean streets. Dirt does not look nice. And germs can grow in dirty places.

Communities try to stop pollution. They may also have people who clean streets, collect garbage, and pick up trash.

What do you do to help keep your community clean?

People in communities need to stay
healthy. Doctors, nurses, dentists, and
druggists help us to be healthy. They also
help us to get better if we get sick.

Do you live near a hospital or clinic?
There may be other health care places in
your community.

We all need energy for hot water, cooking, heating, and cooling. We also need energy for light and other electric things. Cars, trucks, and work machines need energy, too.

We get energy from gas, oil, coal, and electricity. We are learning how to get energy from the sun.

HIGH PRESSURE
TURBINE
STEAM PRESSURE 2400 PSI
STEAM TEMPERATURE 1005°F

People in communities need to move about.

To go a short way you can walk or ride your bike.

What do you do when you want to go a long way? Maybe you will go in a car, bus, train, boat, or airplane. These help people get places faster.

People in communities need to talk to each other.

It is easy to talk with your neighbor.

What do you do when you want to talk to someone far away? Maybe you will use the telephone. Maybe you will write a letter.

You can learn about your community from newspapers, television, and the radio.

People in communities need to have rules.

Sometimes we make the rules ourselves. Sometimes we choose a few people to make the rules for all.

Communities work best when we all follow the rules.

People in communities like to feel
safe.

The police protect us. Fire fighters
put out fires. Emergency people help us,
too. They are there when we need them.

A long time ago, pioneers left their communities to go live in new places.

At first they were all alone. They had to do everything by themselves.

Then they were joined by more pioneers. People began to do things together. Soon they made new communities.

Communities grow when people work together. There are many kinds of communities.

What kind of community do you live in?